**Published By Adam Gilbin**

**@ Alan Heldt**

Change Your Habits: How to Replace Your

Bad Habits With New Ones

**All Right RESERVED**

ISBN 978-87-94477-65-9

# TABLE OF CONTENTS

Chapter 1 ................................................................. 1

Identifying And Choosing Habits ........................... 1

Chapter 2 ............................................................... 25

Identifying Key Tiny Habits For Personal Growth 25

Self-Assessment For Targeted Behavior
Modification......................................................... 25

Chapter 3 ............................................................... 33

Millionaire Habits.................................................. 33

Chapter 4 ............................................................... 49

The Habit Cycle: Trigger, Routine, Reward.......... 49

Chapter 5 ............................................................... 53

Optimizing Your Environment For Habit Success 53

# CHAPTER 1

## IDENTIFYING AND CHOOSING HABITS

In the quest for personal growth and transformation, one of the foundational steps is to identify and choose the right habits. While it may seem straightforward, the process of pinpointing these habits requires introspection, goal setting, and a clear understanding of your values and priorities. In this section, we will delve into the art and science of habit selection, helping you navigate the path toward habits that align with your aspirations and values. Here are guidelines for identifying and choosing the right habits.

**Self-Reflection and Goal-Setting**

Defining Your Goals and Objectives

Before embarking on the journey of habit formation, it's essential to have a clear destination in mind. In this chapter, we'll explore the importance of setting specific, measurable, achievable, relevant, and time-bound (SMART) goals. By defining what you want to achieve in different areas of your life, you'll gain clarity on the habits that can propel you toward those objectives.

**How to Set SMART Goals**

Setting SMART goals is a powerful technique that provides clarity, focus, and a clear path to achieving your objectives. "SMART" is an acronym that stands for Specific, Measurable, Achievable, Relevant, and Time-bound. These criteria serve as a framework for creating well-defined and actionable goals. Let's break down each element of SMART goals.

   **Specific**

Setting a SMART goal starts with being 'Specific.' Your goal should be clear and precise, leaving no room for ambiguity. To make your goal specific, ask yourself the following questions:

What exactly do I want to achieve?

Why is this goal important to me?

Who is involved?

Where will this goal be accomplished?

What are the requirements and constraints?

Example of a non-specific goal: "I want to get better at my job."

Example of a specific goal: "I want to improve my customer service skills by attending a communication workshop to increase customer satisfaction scores by 10% in the next three months."

## 2. Measurable

A measurable goal provides a concrete way to track your progress and determine when you've successfully achieved it. To make your goal measurable, consider:

How will I measure or evaluate my progress?

What are the quantifiable indicators of success?

What is the target or desired outcome?

An example of a non-measurable goal: "I want to lose weight."

Example of a measurable goal: "I want to lose 15 pounds in the next six months by following a healthy diet and exercising for at least 30 minutes five days a week."

**3. Achievable**

Setting an achievable goal should be realistic and attainable given your current resources, skills, and constraints. To assess if your goal is achievable, ask yourself the following questions:

Do I have the necessary resources (time, money, knowledge) to achieve this goal?

Is this goal realistic given my other commitments and priorities?

Can I realistically reach this goal based on my current capabilities?

Example of a non-achievable goal: "I want to become a billionaire by next year."

Example of an achievable goal: "I want to increase my annual savings by 10% by cutting unnecessary expenses and investing wisely."

**4. Relevant**

A relevant goal should align with your values, long-term objectives, and broader life plans. To determine if your goal is relevant:

Does this goal make sense in the context of my life and aspirations?

Will achieving this goal contribute to my overall happiness and well-being?

Is it the right time to pursue this goal?

Example of a non-relevant goal: "I want to learn to play the guitar when my true passion is painting."

Example of a relevant goal: "I want to take advanced painting classes to improve my skills and prepare for an art exhibition in six months."

**5. Time-bound (T):**

Setting a deadline or timeframe creates a sense of urgency and motivation for your goal. To make your goal time-bound, consider the following:

When do I want to achieve this goal?

Is there a specific date or time frame by which I aim to complete it?

What are the milestones or checkpoints along the way?

An example of a non-time-bound goal: "I want to write a novel."

Example of a time-bound goal: "I want to complete the first draft of my novel, consisting of 80,000 words, within 12 months."

Once you've applied the SMART criteria to your goal, you'll have a clear, actionable, and well-defined objective. Writing down your SMART goal can further solidify your commitment to it. Remember to periodically review and adjust your goals as circumstances change, and as you make progress toward achieving them. SMART goals are not static; they can evolve with your journey toward success.

**Identifying Areas for Improvement**

In the journey of goal-setting, identifying areas for improvement and enhancing self-awareness is a critical step in personal growth and development. Here are some strategies to help you identify areas that may need improvement, as well as techniques for self-reflection and self-assessment:

### Self-Reflection Techniques:

Self-reflection is the process of looking inward to gain insight into your thoughts, feelings, and behaviors. Here are some techniques to facilitate self-reflection:

**Journaling**: Regularly write in a journal to record your thoughts, emotions, and experiences. Reflect on your day, your reactions to various situations, and your goals. Journaling can help you identify patterns and areas where you want to improve.

Mindfulness Meditation:

Practicing mindfulness can help you become more aware of your thoughts and emotions. By observing your thoughts without judgment, you can gain clarity about your strengths and weaknesses.

Daily Review:

Take a few minutes at the end of each day to review your actions, decisions, and interactions. Consider what went well and what could have been handled differently.

Feedback Seeking:

Actively seek feedback from trusted friends, family members, mentors, or colleagues. They can provide valuable insights into your strengths and areas where you might need improvement.

SWOT Analysis:

Apply the SWOT (Strengths, Weaknesses, Opportunities, and Threats) analysis framework to yourself. Identify your strengths and weaknesses in various aspects of your life, and consider opportunities for growth and potential threats to your progress.

**2. Self-Assessment Strategies:**

Self-assessment involves using specific tools or methods to evaluate your skills, personality traits, values, and interests. Here are some strategies for self-assessment:

Personality Assessments:

Take personality assessments like the Myers-Briggs Type Indicator (MBTI), the Big Five Personality Test, or the Enneagram to gain insights into your personality traits, preferences, and tendencies.

**Strengths-Based Assessment:**

Discover your strengths and talents through assessments like the Clifton Strengths or VIA Character Strengths. Focusing on your strengths can guide your personal development efforts.

**Skills Inventory**: Create a list of your skills, both hard (e.g., technical skills) and soft (e.g., communication, leadership). Assess which skills you excel in and which you'd like to develop further.

Values Assessment:

Identify your core values by considering what principles and beliefs are most important to you. Aligning your life choices with your values can lead to greater satisfaction and purpose.

Interests and Passions:

Reflect on your interests, hobbies, and passions. What activities bring you joy and fulfillment? Understanding your passions can guide you toward more fulfilling pursuits.

### 3. Seeking External Feedback:

Sometimes, others can help provide valuable insights that you might not see in yourself. Consider seeking feedback from the following:

**Mentors and Coaches:**

A mentor or coach can offer guidance and constructive feedback on your personal and professional development.

**Peer Feedback:**

Colleagues or peers can provide insights into your work style, collaboration skills, and areas for improvement.

**360-Degree Feedback:**

In a professional setting, a 360-degree feedback process involves gathering feedback from supervisors, subordinates, peers, and self-assessment. This comprehensive feedback can offer a well-rounded view of your performance.

**4. Continuous Learning:**

Stay open to learning and acquiring new knowledge. Read books, take courses, attend workshops, and seek experiences that challenge you and expose you to new perspectives.

**5. Set Specific Goals:**

Once you've identified areas for improvement, set specific and actionable goals to work on those areas. Use the SMART goal framework mentioned earlier to create clear and achievable objectives.

Remember that self-awareness is an ongoing process. Regularly revisit your self-assessment and self-reflection practices to track your progress and adjust your goals as needed. Embrace self-awareness as a tool for personal growth and a foundation for making informed decisions and positive changes in your life.

**Prioritizing Your Habits**

Prioritizing your habits can be a critical step in getting an outstanding result. That small habit can change the whole narrative for you. Stop trying to do everything at a time, and prioritize yourself. Know the tasks that are more important to you and follow them. This also goes with achieving a goal. If you have 5 goals to achieve, and you want to achieve them all at the same time, then, you don't have a goal, then you're not prioritizing. Let's take a look at the Pareto's principle

The Pareto Principle: Focusing On the Vital Few

The Pareto Principle, often known as the 80/20 rule, asserts that a small percentage of effort often leads to a large percentage of results. In this chapter, we'll explore how this principle applies to habit formation. By focusing on a select few high-impact habits, you can maximize your effectiveness and avoid spreading yourself too thin.

The Pareto Principle, also known as the 80/20 rule or the principle of factor sparsity, is a concept that suggests that, in many situations, a significant portion of the results or effects come from a relatively small percentage of the causes or inputs. The principle is named after the Italian economist Vilfredo Pareto, who observed in the early 20th century that approximately 80% of Italy's land was owned by 20% of the population. This observation has since been applied to a wide range of fields and contexts.

In the context of habit formation and personal development, the Pareto Principle has a profound impact. Here's how it relates to habit formation:

Focus on High-Impact Habits:

The Pareto Principle suggests that a minority of your habits will likely contribute to the majority of your results. In other words, a small number of habits have the potential to make a significant impact on your life. As you work to build new habits or improve existing ones, it's beneficial to identify and prioritize these high-impact habits.

**Efficiency and Prioritization:**

By recognizing the Pareto Principle, you can prioritize your efforts more effectively. Instead of trying to change everything at once, focus on the vital few habits that are most likely to move the needle toward your goals. This approach can save you time and energy while delivering meaningful results.

**Achieving More with Less:**

The Pareto Principle encourages a minimalist and efficient approach to habit formation. Rather than overwhelming yourself with numerous habits to change or goals to achieve, concentrate your efforts on a select few. This approach can reduce the risk of burnout and increase your chances of success.

**Ongoing Assessment:**

Regularly assess your habits and their impact on your life. Are there habits that consistently deliver positive results? Are there habits that consume time and energy without commensurate benefits? By conducting these assessments, you can adjust and refine your habit-building strategy.

**Compound Effect:**

The principle aligns with the idea that small changes can lead to significant cumulative effects over time. High-impact habits, when consistently practiced, can compound and lead to substantial improvements in your life. This compounding effect is often referred to as the "aggregation of marginal gains."

**Applying the Principles:**

To apply the Pareto Principle to habit formation, start by identifying the habits that are most likely to drive your desired outcomes. These could be habits related to health, productivity, relationships, or any area of your life. Once identified, focus on mastering and maintaining these habits while keeping a watchful eye on their impact.

Keep in mind that the exact distribution of cause-and-effect relationships may not always conform to an 80/20 ratio, but the underlying concept remains valuable. The Pareto Principle underscores the importance of strategic thinking and efficient allocation of your efforts when it comes to habit formation, personal growth, and goal achievement. By concentrating on the vital few habits that matter most, you can make substantial progress toward your aspirations.

**Creating a Habit Hierarchy**

Not all habits are created equal, and some may have a more profound impact on your life than others. In this section, we'll guide you through the process of creating a habit hierarchy—a prioritized list of habits based on their significance to your goals and values. This hierarchy will serve as a roadmap for your habit-building journey, ensuring you allocate your time and energy to the habits that matter most.

Creating a habit hierarchy is a valuable exercise in prioritizing and organizing your habits to maximize their impact on your life. This hierarchy helps you focus on the most critical habits that will contribute significantly to your goals and personal growth. Here's a step-by-step guide on how to create a habit hierarchy:

### Define Your Goals:

Before you can create a habit hierarchy, you need to have clear goals in mind. Identify the specific areas of your life where you want to see improvement. These could include health and fitness, career, relationships, personal development, or any other aspect that is important to you. Make sure your goals are SMART (Specific, Measurable, Achievable, Relevant, and Time-bound).

**List Your Current Habits:**

Create a comprehensive list of your current habits, both positive and negative. These can include daily routines, behaviors, and activities that you engage in regularly. Be honest and thorough in your assessment.

### 3. Access Each Habit:

Evaluate each habit on your list in terms of its impact on your goals and well-being. Ask yourself the following questions:

How does this habit contribute to or hinder my progress toward my goals?

Is this habit aligned with my values and priorities?

Does this habit have a positive or negative impact on my health, happiness, or productivity?

Is this habit essential, or can I live without it?

## 4. Categorize Your Habits:

Group your habits into categories based on their relevance to your goals and values. You may have categories like "High-Impact Habits," "Moderate-Impact Habits," and "Low-Impact Habits." The high-impact category should contain habits that have the most significant positive impact on your goals.

## 5. Rank Your Habits:

Within each category, rank your habits by their importance and effectiveness in helping you achieve your goals. The habit at the top of the list should be the one you consider the most crucial for your progress. Continue ranking the habits within each category until you have a clear hierarchy.

## 6. Create Your Habit Hierarchy:

Now that you have ranked your habits, it's time to create your habit hierarchy. Your hierarchy will typically consist of three tiers:

### Tier 1: High-Impact Habits:

These are your top-priority habits, the ones that have the most significant impact on your goals and well-being. Focus your energy on developing and maintaining these habits.

### Tier 2: Moderate-Impact Habits:

These habits are important but not as critical as those in Tier 1. They still contribute to your progress, and you should give them attention once your Tier 1 habits are firmly established.

### Tier 3: Low-Impact Habits:

These habits have minimal impact on your goals or may even be counterproductive. Consider eliminating or minimizing these habits to free up time and resources for your higher-priority habits.

**7. Develop an Action Plan:**

For each habit in your hierarchy, create an action plan. Define the specific steps and routines you will follow to establish and maintain these habits. Include details like when, where, and how you will practice them.

**8. Monitor Your Progress:**

Regularly assess your progress with your habit hierarchy. Track how well you are adhering to your high-impact habits and adjust your efforts as needed. Celebrate your successes and learn from any setbacks.

**9. Adapt and Evolve:**

Your habit hierarchy is not set in stone. It should evolve as you make progress toward your goals and as your priorities change. Periodically reassess your habits and update your hierarchy to reflect your current circumstances and aspirations.

Creating a habit hierarchy helps you stay focused on what matters most in your journey of personal growth and goal achievement. By concentrating your efforts on the high-impact habits at the top of your hierarchy, you can make substantial strides toward realizing your aspirations.

## Chapter 2

## Identifying Key Tiny Habits for Personal Growth

### Self-Assessment for Targeted Behavior Modification

Behavioral health is an important element of total well-being, and recognizing your habits and patterns is an important start toward making good changes. This self-evaluation is intended to assist you in evaluating your present behaviors and identifying areas for targeted adjustment.Follow the steps below to acquire insight into your behaviors and get started on the path to positive behavior change.

### Step1:Examine Current Behaviors

Consider your everyday routines, behaviors, and reactions to different circumstances. Take into account both good and bad actions that may have an influence on your well-being.

**Step 2:Determine Triggers**

Investigate the triggers that cause particular actions.Are your behaviors influenced by specific events, emotions, or environmental factors? Understanding these triggers is essential for focused behavior change.

**Step 3:Evaluate Emotional Reactions**

Examine your emotional reactions to various scenarios.Recognize tension, worry, or other emotion patterns connected with certain behaviors.This insight can help you create better coping methods.

**Step 4:Specify the desired changes**

Outline the behaviors you wish to change in detail. Set reasonable, attainable objectives and be precise about the improvements you want to achieve.Divide larger ambitions into smaller, more achievable tasks.

**Step 5: Assess Progress**

Create a method for keeping track of your progress. Keeping a diary, utilizing a monitoring tool, or participating in frequent self-reflection might all be part of this. Monitoring your development gives you useful feedback and incentive.

**Step 6: Seek Help**

Think about enlisting the help of a trustworthy friend, family member, or mental health expert in your journey. Support may be a strong motivator and might offer you with new insights on your conduct.

**Step 7: Use Positive Reinforcement.**

Determine positive reinforcements that may be used to encourage desirable actions. Positive reinforcement may boost motivation, whether it's rewarding yourself for hitting goals or recognizing your efforts.

**Step 8: Learn from Mistakes**

Recognize that setbacks are a normal aspect of changing your behavior. Instead of perceiving them as failures, consider them chances to learn and improve your strategy. Analyze what caused the setback and plan how to overcome similar obstacles in the future.

**Step 9: Modify Your Strategies**

Be open-minded in your approach. If some solutions aren't producing the intended outcomes, be open to adapt and try other approaches. Behavioral transformation is a fluid process that may need trial and error.

Step 10: Rejoice in Your Victories

Recognize and appreciate every achievement, no matter how minor. Recognizing accomplishments promotes positive behavior and improves confidence, resulting in a positive transformation cycle.

By conducting this self-evaluation and following these steps, you empower yourself to make focused and significant behavioral changes, ultimately leading to improved overall well-being and mental health.

Remember that the path to good transformation is an ongoing one, and every effort you make is a step in the right way.

**Selecting Habits with Maximum Impact**

Choosing habits with the greatest impact is an important part of behavioral health since it has a direct impact on overall well-being. Consider the following elements while identifying habits for maximum impact:

Personalization entails tailoring behaviors to a person's interests, strengths, and lifestyle. What works for one person may not work for another, so choosing habits that correspond with personal beliefs and aspirations is critical.

**1. Begin Small:**

To lay the groundwork for success, start with simple habits. Small, regular adjustments are more likely to be sustained and can eventually lead to bigger, beneficial transformations.

**2. Prioritize Mental Well-Being:**

Include behaviors that promote mental health, such as mindfulness techniques, deep breathing exercises, and regular times of self-reflection. A healthy mind is the cornerstone of good health.

Physical activity has a significant influence on both physical and mental health. Choose activities that are both entertaining and feasible to ensure long-term compliance.

**3. Nutrition:**

Choose a well-balanced and healthy diet.Small changes, such as drinking more water or eating more fruits and vegetables, may have a big impact on your overall health.

**4.Quality Sleep:**

Make excellent sleep hygiene a priority.Create a pleasant sleeping environment and stick to the necessary amount of sleep each night for improved cognitive performance and emotional well-being.

**5.Positive**

Relationships and Social ties: Encourage positive relationships and social ties. Participating in activities with supportive friends and family can help with emotional resilience and a sense of belonging.

**6.Use of Mindful Technology:**

Be deliberate in your use of technology. Set screen time limits, particularly before bedtime, to encourage better sleep and minimize stress.

Develop efficient time management techniques to decrease stress and boost productivity. To maintain a healthy work-life balance, prioritize tasks, set reasonable objectives, and take pauses.

**7. Continual Learning:**

Make continual learning a habit. Engaging in lifelong learning, whether via reading, online courses, or skill development, can improve cognitive function and create a sense of success.

Remember that consistency is the key. Building habits that have the greatest impact takes time, and the emphasis should be on gradual, long-term adjustments that correspond with individual needs and goals.

# CHAPTER 3

# MILLIONAIRE HABITS

Who doesn't have dreams of being a millionaire? We all wish we could get to that point in life, and some people actually make it. Of course, there are always going to be millionaires that get where they are because their family has money, but that isn't the case in every situation. A lot of millionaires these days are self-made, and there's no reason you can't be the same way.

When you practice millionaire habits, you're giving yourself plenty of opportunity to earn a lot of money and succeed in life without having to make difficult changes to do it. Millionaire habits are a little tougher to enforce than normal, everyday good habits, but when you spend time working on them, you'll see the results quickly.

**What makes a millionaire habit?**

Millionaire habits are the good behaviors you can add into your daily routine to help you make the most out of life. Millionaires often earn their money the hard way, and self-made millionaires are getting more and more common in modern society. When you practice these habits, you can work your way up the economic ladder too. You'll see changes in no time, and you'll be on your way toward being a self-made millionaire yourself.

So what makes these habits so different from any others? They're all good habits, and they're all designed to help you improve yourself in some way. Money isn't everything, and you can't expect to go out into the world and make money without first improving yourself as a person. The more you do to work on yourself, the better off you'll be in the workplace and in the rest of your life, too.

**Read often and learn as much as you can**

Being well-read is the first step toward a better life. If you set aside half an hour every day to read something, you'll learn more about how to communicate with others both verbally and in writing. You'll discover words you've never encountered before, and you will have more to talk about with the people you work with too. Reading anything is good practice for communication, but try to read novels instead of magazines or web sites whenever possible to get the best results.

Try to learn something new every week, too. Even if it's something you'll never use again, look up a topic and see what you can find out about it. You might not ever need to know how to use a water softener, for example, but it might be interesting to find out what they do! You never know when this new information will come in handy down the line.

**Stay up to date on current information**

Current information is always important, and it's a great way to break the ice and do some networking in a work environment. Current events don't always have to be political or even that important, but it's a good idea to pay attention to these as well. You can also pepper your reading with fun things like the latest celebrity gossip, to give yourself an in with just about any conversation

**Make lists**

We've already talked about the importance of making lists in general, but when it comes to working toward becoming a self-made millionaire, lists are crucial. You can't become successful without keeping track of your work, your finances, and your time, so be sure to handle your lists in the most organized fashion possible to stay on top of everything.

Use separate notebooks and differently-colored highlighters or pens to keep track of different parts of your life. Keep a calendar with plenty of notes, so you never forget when important deadlines are coming up. It's also a good idea to list out contacts that can help you get ahead in the workplace, and keep them on hand for those times when you need to do a little extra networking.

**Be careful with your finances**

Plan your finances carefully to put your money to work for you. Don't spend all over the place, and plan a budget that you can follow. It's important not to stretch your budget so thin that it's impossible to stick to it for even a single month, but to keep from giving yourself too much wiggle room as well. When you plan out your budget carefully and pay attention to your finances, you'll find it much easier to put aside money in the long run.

Spread your money throughout many different areas as well. If you can make money in more than one way, by all means, do it! You can hold down a regular job and work on something else on the side, such as selling crafts online or baked goods locally. Be sure to put some money in savings and try some in stocks as well. The more you spread your finances, the more return you will eventually see. It will take time and patience, but you will be a self-made millionaire eventually when you stick to these great habits.

### INCLUDE EXERCISE IN YOUR ROUTINE

**Similar to your morning routine, you don't have to take up marathons to be successful. When building good habits, the key to making yours work is sustainability. You're not trying to do something big just for that one time. You're trying to form habits that you can introduce into**

**your life permanently.**

If you already have enough exercise in your routine, then you're already halfway there. But if you think you could do more, something as small as a 20-minute walk twice a week can make a difference in your world.

That level of exercise does wonders for your productivity, mental health, and your physical health. Whether it's walking, running, weight-lifting, or swimming, injecting a small level of exercise into your weekly routine will help you on the road to success. You have to remember that it is all about the mind, the BODY, and your soul, which is how you feel in the inside.

What do Cher, Warren Buffet, and OKCupid founder, Christian Rudder, all have in common? While you might have guessed that they're professionals at the top of their game, it's not the only similarity. The truth is that they all have an even bigger commonality among them. They all work out and consider it integral to their success. They aren't the only ones, either. Entrepreneurs like Richard Branson (who's started over 400 companies) have long known that regular physical activity, may it be running, lifting, or yoga, can provide you with up to four extra hours of productivity every day. Even President Barack Obama -- a slacker until he began running three miles a day as a young man -- makes time for 45-minute workouts before tackling his duties. Working hard and working out go hand-in-hand. Here are five reasons why:

1. You'll benefit from schedules and goals.

It is no secret that Rhodes Scholars are amongst the most accomplished, organized and successful people in the world. Why? The Rhodes Scholar program at Oxford's University takes the sports accomplishments of their candidates as seriously as they take the academic ones. Graduates of the University have well balanced lives, with both intellectual and physical accomplishments. They are good habit-making machines!

If you're not already setting schedules for yourself, working out is a great way to build that habit. Set time aside and give yourself goals you're actively working towards, whether it's losing weight or running a certain distance. Practicing discipline as you workout and seeing the results will help you carry that into the desired niche of interest you may have when it comes to your career goals. You must create professional checkpoints to work towards. Try your best to avoid getting frustrated if you don't get the results you want right away. Results may take time.

2. It'll build your brain to learn self-control and help break bad habits.

After a long day of work, it's tempting to crash in front of the TV and eat or drink your frustrations away. You worked hard and may think you deserve it now, but have you asked yourself what you deserve in the long run? It can be hard to connect with your deeper needs when you're always working or distracted from your true desires. Personally, I was susceptible to a lack of focus that made me jump from one thing to another. I got easily distracted and fell prey to a lack of discipline.

That's one of the best things about exercise. It puts your mind in contact with your body and makes them unified. Taking those few minutes out of your day to find work outs that you would most likely follow through. It'll help you do a rundown on what you really need, in order for you, to accomplish what you want. It allows you to collect your thoughts and instills a sense of direction instead of letting you indulge yourself into things that may be avoidable. It's really the best way to break any destructive habits that stand in your way. It allows all the pressures of responsibility -- and the desire for escape that goes with it -- to slide away, replacing that pressure with a one-on-one conversation with yourself.

Knowledge is power, and knowing what you need makes you smarter, more resilient, and better able to create better habits moving forward. Therefore, learning will become the superpower to everything known demand through your own manifestations and desires.

3. You'll stay competitive with others, and yourself.

It is often publicized that many of the Fortune 500 and the most innovative companies in the world including Google, Apple, and even Deloitte have onsite exercise facilities. The reason is simple: making exercise easily accessible eliminates an excuse and encourages everyone in the company to use the facilities. In turn, this exercise makes everyone at the company sharper and more competitive. Therefore, the company itself will be sharper and more competitive. Even "old world" companies, like big banks and accounting firms, are building exercise rooms into their new facilities because they know it leads to powerful results.

As we all know, work can be so frustrating. You may be pushing yourself to do the best you can, but whether it's negative supervisors, gossipy co-workers, or just feeling stuck doing the same thing over and over again, it becomes difficult to stay engaged at work when this feeling strikes. If you fall victim to this thinking, your career will suffer. It's always good to shake it up and find a way to relieve the stress. Regular exercise not only keeps you in the fight, but gets you working harder, better, and smarter. Aren't these the true components that we desire in our life in order to succeed in what we want?

After all, if you want to be the best, you have to work harder and harder to be your best self every day. Keep pushing yourself to climb and compete, both physically and mentally. As you do, you'll see that the negative voices and thoughts disappearing. The naysayers will fall to the wayside as you regain control of your mood, your body, your career, and your life. Don't ever accept limitations. Keep working, and don't give up -- especially not on yourself. You are limitless.

4. It builds self esteem for a healthier you both inside and out.

Michael Strahan, a football prodigy, once said, "We're our own worst enemies. You doubt yourself more than anybody ever will. If you can get past that, you will be successful."

Working out can not only decrease stress, but teaches you that you can excel beyond the limitations you've set for yourself. It builds your body and mind into a sharper tool. Just by knowing and feeling that does amazing wonders for your self-esteem. Switching gears from "I can't" to "I can and I will" is an unbelievable change of perspective, and fully believing that allows you to overcome what you once thought was impossible.

5. You'll work smarter, not harder.

Having a regular commitment outside the office can be incredibly necessary. Just as you can burn out from over-exercise, you can hit a point of diminishing returns if you stay much longer than eight hours at the office. Scheduled or spontaneous workout time can help you make the most of your work time by keeping you aware that when it's time to stop, it's really quitting time. It's comforting to know that even if you're not at work, you're building a more focused, productive you. Doing it with loved ones, friends, or even co-workers has the added benefit of bringing everyone together and maybe even solving a few problems on the court! Don't shy away from putting your health and happiness first!

Remember, this advice is not about getting bikini-ready or becoming an Adonis. It's about getting in shape, inside and out, to tackle the most important challenges in your life. It's about creating patterns in your life that bring about the best in you as much as possible. After all, politicians and celebrities aren't fictional characters. They're real people who have seen real results, and that can be you too! Give your body the attention it deserves, and your professional life will follow suit. If you want to build a strong career, you'll need the strength to build it. One of those strengths come from your physical being.

## Chapter 4

**The Habit Cycle: Trigger, Routine, Reward**

Understanding the Secret Engine of Habits

Now that you have a general understanding of habits, it's time to take a deep dive into their inner workings. Habits are like little engines that drive our daily behavior, and understanding the habit cycle is key to changing them effectively.

The Habit Cycle in Detail

The habit cycle is made up of three interconnected elements:

1. Trigger: This is the starting point. The trigger is what starts the habit. It can be anything that activates your mind and prepares it for action. Triggers can be divided into two main categories:

- External triggers: Things outside of you, like an alarm, a notification on your cell phone or even the smell of food.

- Internal triggers: Feelings, emotions or thoughts that trigger a habit, such as stress, sadness or boredom.

Identifying triggers is essential to understanding why we perform certain habits in certain situations.

2. Routine: The routine is the part of the habit that you do automatically in response to the trigger. It's habitual behavior that you perform almost without thinking. For example, when feeling stressed (trigger), you may resort to eating a snack (routine).

3. Reward: The reward is what you get or feel after completing the routine. It is responsible for reinforcing the habit cycle. In the example above, the reward might be a temporary feeling of relief from stress. The reward satisfies a specific need or desire.

Example of a Habit Cycle

Let's look at a common example of a habit loop: compulsively checking your cell phone. The trigger can be a notification (external trigger) or a feeling of boredom (internal trigger). The routine involves taking out your cell phone and checking messages or social media. The reward can be the instant gratification of seeing a new message or receiving a quick dose of entertainment.

Modifying Habits

Understanding the habit loop allows us to modify our behaviors. If you want to change a habit, you can:

- Identify the Trigger: Try to recognize what triggers the habit. Once you know the trigger, you can take steps to avoid or replace it.

- Restructure the Routine: Instead of performing the same usual routine in response to the trigger, try replacing it with a healthier or more positive action.

- Reward Yourself in a Healthy Way: Find alternative rewards that satisfy your needs in a healthier way. This helps reinforce the new habit.

Conclusion

The habit loop is the foundation of our understanding of how habits work. By taking apart and analyzing the triggers, routines, and rewards of your own habits, you'll be one step closer to consciously shaping your behavior. In the next chapter, we'll explore how to identify bad habits and begin the journey toward positive change.

Remember that the power is in your hands to direct the habit loop toward desired results. We will continue to explore this exciting journey of self-discovery and personal growth.

# CHAPTER 5

# OPTIMIZING YOUR ENVIRONMENT FOR HABIT SUCCESS

Creating an environment that supports your habit-building efforts is a crucial component of success. Your surroundings have a significant impact on your behavior, making it essential to optimize them to facilitate habit formation. In this chapter, we delve into the concept of environmental optimization and provide practical guidance on how to set up your surroundings for habit success.

## The Influence of Environment on Habits

Your physical and social environment plays a powerful role in shaping your habits. Here's how:

1. Cues and Triggers:

Environmental cues and triggers can prompt specific behaviors. For example, seeing your running shoes by the door can trigger the habit of going for a run.

2. Accessibility:

The ease with which you can access certain items or activities in your environment can either support or hinder habit formation. If healthy snacks are readily available in your kitchen, you're more likely to make nutritious choices.

**3. Social Norms:**

Your social environment and the behaviors of those around you can influence your habits. If your friends prioritize fitness and invite you to join them for workouts, you're more likely to adopt an active lifestyle.

**4. Distractions:**

Clutter, noise, and distractions in your environment can disrupt your focus and hinder habit-building efforts. A tidy, organized space can promote concentration and productivity.

**Optimizing Your Environment for Habit Success**

To optimize your surroundings for habit success, consider the following strategies:

**1. Identify Habit-Supportive Elements:**

Evaluate your environment and identify elements that can support your desired habit. This could include placing your guitar in a visible spot if you want to practice more or organizing your workspace for improved productivity.

**2. Eliminate or Minimize Triggers for Unwanted Habits:**

Identify triggers that prompt undesirable habits and work on minimizing or eliminating them. For instance, if you're trying to reduce screen time, consider placing your phone out of sight during work hours.

**3. Create a Dedicated Space:**

If possible, allocate a specific space for habit-related activities. This can help establish a clear association between the space and the habit. For example, designate a corner of your home for reading or meditation.

**4. Make Necessary Tools Accessible:**

Ensure that the tools or resources required for your habit are easily accessible. If you want to write daily, keep your journal or laptop within reach.

**5. Customize Your Environment:**

Personalize your environment to align with your habits. Decorate your workout area with motivational posters or set up a cozy reading nook with your favorite books.

**6. Social Support:**

Surround yourself with supportive individuals who share your goals or encourage your habits. Seek out communities, online or offline, that align with your interests.

**7. Minimize Distractions:**

Identify distractions in your environment and take steps to minimize them. This could involve organizing your workspace, silencing notifications, or creating designated quiet times.

**8. Adapt to Changing Needs:**

Be adaptable and adjust your environment as your needs and habits evolve. What works for one habit may not be suitable for another, so remain open to changes.

By optimizing your surroundings for habit success, you create an environment that encourages and reinforces positive behaviors. Your environment becomes a silent but powerful ally in your habit-building journey, making it easier to stay consistent and achieve your goals.

**Dealing with Habit Disruptors: Overcoming Challenges on Your Journey**

Building and sustaining habits is rarely a linear process. Along the way, you'll encounter habit disruptors—obstacles and challenges that threaten to derail your progress. In this chapter, we explore various habit disruptors and provide strategies for overcoming them, ensuring that you can navigate the bumps on your journey toward lasting change.

## Common Habit Disruptors

Habit disruptors can manifest in different forms, and they may include:

### 1. External Factors:

Life events, such as job changes, relocation, or family emergencies, can disrupt your routine and make it challenging to stick to your habits.

### 2. Procrastination and Laziness:

Moments of procrastination or simply feeling lazy can tempt you to skip your habit for the day.

### 3. Lack of Motivation:

Motivation naturally fluctuates, and there will be days when you don't feel particularly inspired to engage in your habit.

### 4. Stress and Emotional Triggers:

Stress, anxiety, and emotional triggers can lead to the abandonment of healthy habits in favor of coping mechanisms like emotional eating or excessive screen time.

### 5. External Temptations:

External temptations, such as junk food or distractions like social media, can divert your attention and hinder habit execution.

Strategies for Dealing with Habit Disruptors

To effectively address habit disruptors, consider these strategies:

### 1. Anticipate and Plan for Disruptions:

Recognize that disruptions are a natural part of life. Plan ahead for how you'll adapt your habits during challenging periods, such as vacations or busy work weeks.

**2. Break It Down:**

On days when motivation is low, focus on breaking your habit into smaller, more manageable chunks. If you usually run for 30 minutes, commit to just 5 minutes. Often, starting is the hardest part.

**3. Reconnect with Your "Why":**

Revisit the reasons behind your habit. Reconnecting with your "why" can reignite your motivation and remind you why this habit is essential to you.

**4. Implement Accountability:**

Share your goals and progress with an accountability partner or a supportive community. Knowing that someone is watching can boost your commitment.

**5. Develop Resilience Skills:**

Practice resilience techniques, such as mindfulness, meditation, or stress management, to cope with emotional triggers and stress-related disruptors.

**6. Avoid Temptations:**

Minimize exposure to external temptations that can divert your focus. Create an environment that supports your habits and reduces the likelihood of distractions.

**7. Embrace Flexibility:**

Be flexible in your approach. It's okay to adapt your habits or adjust your routine when necessary. What matters is the overall consistency over time.

**8. Track and Reflect:**

Keep a habit journal or use a habit-tracking app to monitor your progress. Regularly reflect on your experiences and learn from past disruptions.

**9. Seek Support:**

Don't hesitate to seek support from friends, family, or professionals if you're struggling with habit disruptors that feel overwhelming.

**10. Reframe Setbacks as Learning Opportunities:**

Instead of viewing disruptions as failures, see them as opportunities to learn and grow. Identify what triggered the disruption and strategize how to handle it better in the future.

Dealing with habit disruptors is an integral part of the habit-building process. It's not about avoiding disruptions altogether but learning how to navigate them effectively. By implementing these strategies and maintaining a resilient mindset, you can overcome challenges and continue progressing toward your habit-related goals.

**How to Make Habits Irresistible**

To make habits irresistible, you can use a combination of strategies to increase their appeal and motivation. Here are some effective techniques:

**Connect With Values:**

Align your habits with your core values and long-term goals. When a habit is meaningful and in harmony with your values, it becomes more compelling.

**Visualize Success:**

Create a vivid mental image of the positive outcomes and benefits of your habit. Visualization can enhance motivation and make the habit more attractive.

**Immediate Rewards:**

Design your habits to offer immediate rewards or benefits. The sooner you experience positive outcomes, the more enticing the habit becomes.

**Use Temptation Bundling:**

Combine a habit you want to develop with something you enjoy. For example, listen to your favorite podcast only while exercising.

**Make It Social:**

Share your habit journey with friends or join a group with similar interests. Social support and accountability can make the habit more engaging.

**Gamify Your Habits:**

Turn your habit into a game with challenges, rewards, and milestones. Gamification adds an element of fun and competition.

**Track Progress Visually:**

Use a habit tracker or visual representation to monitor your progress. Seeing your achievements visually can be motivating.

**Commit Publicly:**

Announce your habit goals to friends, family, or on social media. The fear of not meeting public commitments can drive you to stick with the habit.

**Create a Pleasurable Environment:**

Surround yourself with a pleasant atmosphere when practicing your habit. Play your favorite music during workouts or set up a cozy reading nook for daily reading.

**Positive Self-Talk:**

Replace negative thoughts about the habit with positive affirmations. Encourage yourself and focus on the benefits you'll gain.

**Finding and Fixing Causes of Bad Habits:**

Identifying and addressing the root causes of bad habits is essential for breaking them. Here's how to find and fix the causes:

**Self-Reflection:**

Begin by analyzing your bad habit. What triggers it? What emotions or situations lead to it? Self-awareness is the first step in understanding the cause.

**Identify Triggers:**

Determine the specific cues or triggers that prompt your bad habit. Is it stress, boredom, social pressure, or something else? Recognizing triggers is crucial.

**Replace with Alternatives:**

Find healthier, positive alternatives to satisfy the same needs or triggers that drive your bad habit. For example, if stress triggers overeating, consider stress-reduction techniques like meditation.

**Change Your Environment:**

Modify your surroundings to make it harder to engage in the bad habit. Remove temptations or obstacles that enable the habit.

**Seek Support:**

Share your intention to change with a friend or therapist who can provide guidance, support, and accountability.

**Practice Mindfulness:**

Develop mindfulness techniques to observe your thoughts and urges without acting on them. This helps you gain control over impulsive behaviors.

**Gradual Reduction:**

If quitting the bad habit cold turkey is challenging, consider gradually reducing it over time. Set specific milestones for reducing the habit's frequency.

**Use Habit Reversal Training:**

This technique involves identifying the cues, rewards, and routines of your bad habit and replacing them with healthier alternatives.

**Positive Reinforcement:**

Reward yourself for making progress in breaking the bad habit. Positive reinforcement can strengthen your commitment to change.

**Professional Help:**

If the bad habit is causing significant harm or is deeply ingrained, consider seeking professional assistance, such as therapy or counseling.

Breaking bad habits is a process that may require patience and persistence. Understanding the underlying causes and implementing targeted strategies can significantly increase your chances of successfully replacing bad habits with healthier ones.

www.ingramcontent.com/pod-product-compliance
Lightning Source LLC
LaVergne TN
LVHW010608070526
838199LV00063BA/5108